Nature Up Close™

Bees Up Close

PowerKiDS press™

New York

Katie Franks

Published in 2008 by The Rosen Publishing Group, Inc.
29 East 21st Street, New York, NY 10010

First Edition

Editor: Jennifer Way
Book Design: Kate Laczynski
Photo Researcher: Nicole Pristash

Photo Credits: Cover, pp. 1, 5, 7, 9 (inset) 11, 13, 15, 17, 19, 21, 24 © Studio Stalio; p. 9 (main) © Shutterstock.com; p. 23 by Alessandro Bartolozzi.

Library of Congress Cataloging-in-Publication Data

Franks, Katie.
  Bees up close / Katie Franks. — 1st ed.
      p. cm. — (Nature up close)
  Includes index.
  ISBN 978-1-4042-4137-4 (library binding)
  1. Honeybee—Juvenile literature. I. Title.
  QL568.A6F545 2008
  595.79'9—dc22
                                        2007018165

Manufactured in the United States of America

Contents

This is a honeybee. Bees are known for making honey.

5

A bee has many body parts. Some of these are the **stinger**, the **antennae**, the wings, and the legs.

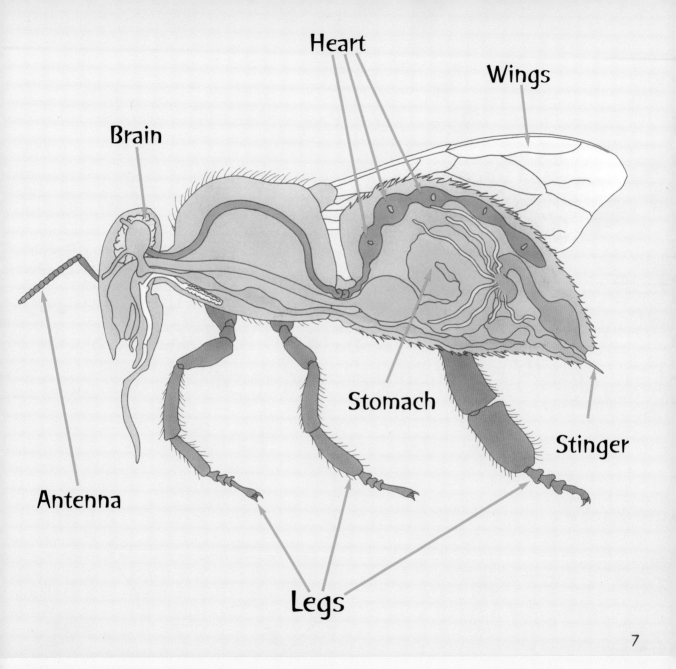

Heart

Wings

Brain

Antenna

Stomach

Stinger

Legs

Bees have a special mouthpart called a **proboscis**. The proboscis is used to help bees eat.

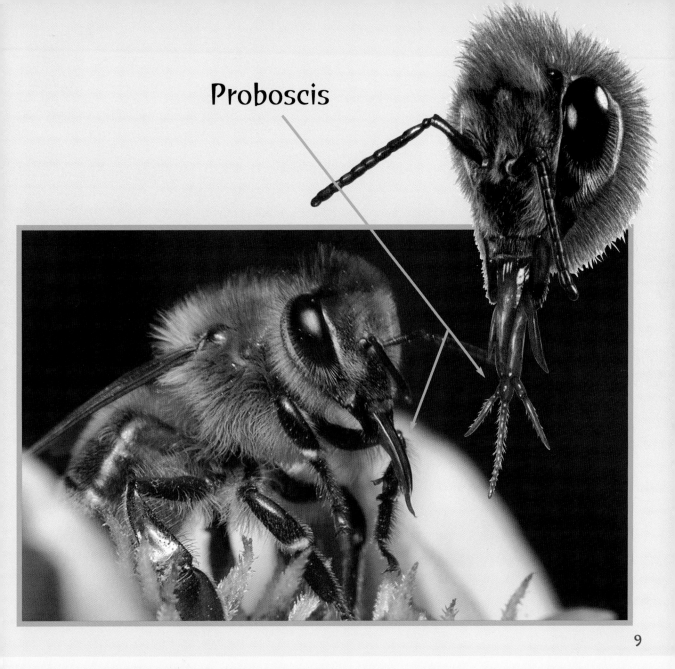

Proboscis

Bees live in a **hive** in a group called a **colony**. The colony has worker bees, drones, and a queen. The queen leads the colony.

Queen

Worker

Drone

11

Worker bees gather nectar and pollen to bring back to the hive. Nectar and pollen are found in flowers.

Worker bees build the hive using a wax that is made by their body. Hives are made up of honeycombs.

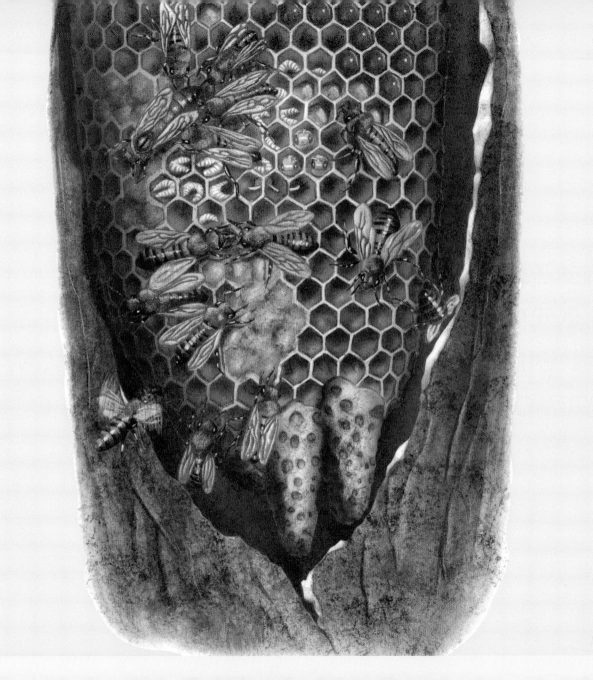

15

Honeycombs can hold honey, bee eggs, or growing bees. In these drawings, you can see how an egg grows into an adult bee.

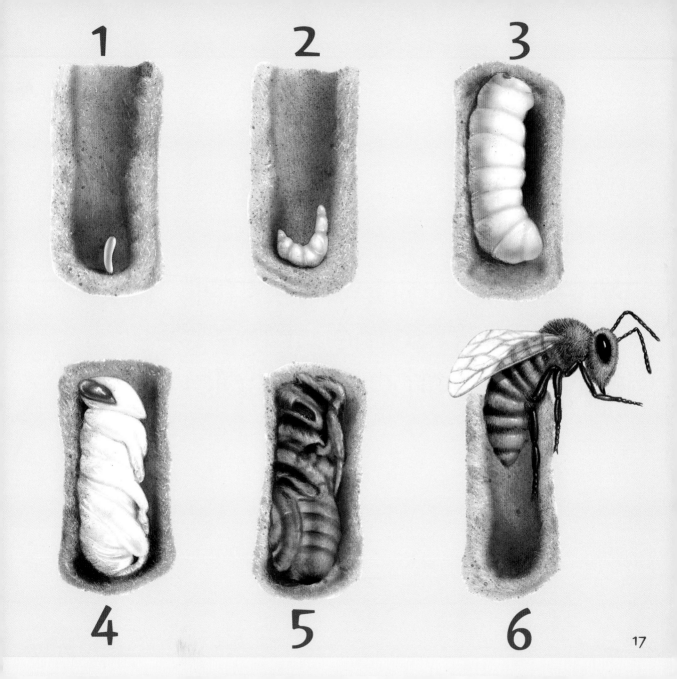

1   2   3

4   5   6

17

When the colony gets full, the queen and some of the bees leave to start a new colony.

19

Beeswax can be made into **candles**. Honey is used as food.

Bees live all around the world. On this map of the world, the places where bees live are shown in brown.

North America

Europe

Asia

South America

Africa

Australia

Words to Know

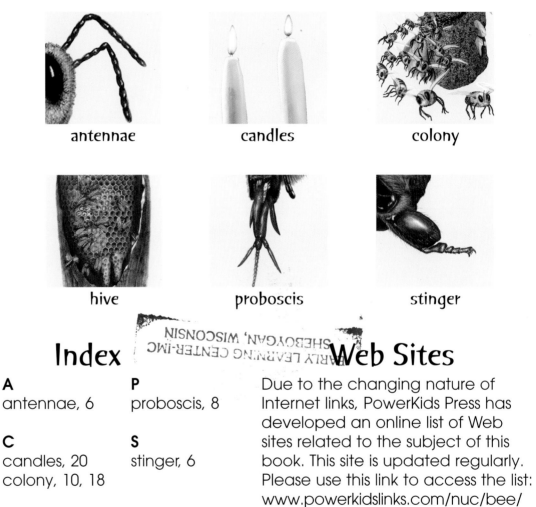

antennae

candles

colony

hive

proboscis

stinger

Web Sites

Due to the changing nature of Internet links, PowerKids Press has developed an online list of Web sites related to the subject of this book. This site is updated regularly. Please use this link to access the list: www.powerkidslinks.com/nuc/bee/